SPA(E

OUR MOON

IAN GRAHAM

FRANKLIN WATTS
LONDON • SYDNEY

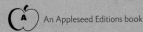 An Appleseed Editions book

First published in Great Britain in 2016
by The Watts Publishing Group

Copyright © 2014 Appleseed Editions

Designed by Guy Callaby
Edited by Mary-Jane Wilkins

Picture acknowledgements
t = top, b = bottom, l = left, r = right
title page O.Bellini; 2-3 FrameAngel;
4 Olga_Phoenix; 5 Jaochainoi; 6 Keith
Publicover/all Shutterstock; 7 Gabriele
Maltinti/Thinkstock; 8-9 NASA/JPL-
Caltech, 8b fluidworkshop; 10 David
Carillet; 11 Procy; 12 bikeriderlondon/
all Shutterstock; 13 JPL/NASA Planetary
Photojournal; 14 NASA; 15 Valerio Pardi/
Shutterstock; 16, 17, 18, 19 NASA;
20 Harm Kruyshaar; 21 Aptyp_koK/
both Shutterstock
Cover t ravl/Shutterstock, b Stocktrek
Images/Thinkstock

Every attempt has been made to clear
copyright. Should there be any inadvertent
omission please apply to the publisher
for rectification.

Dewey number 523.3
HB ISBN 978 1 4451 4912 7

Printed in China

MIX
Paper from
responsible sources
FSC
www.fsc.org   FSC® C104740

Franklin Watts
An imprint of
Hachette Children's Group
Part of The Watts Publishing Group
Carmelite House
50 Victoria Embankment
London EC4Y 0DZ

An Hachette UK Company
www.hachette.co.uk

www.franklinwatts.co.uk

CONTENTS

Our Moon

Some planets have dozens of moons, but the Earth has only one. Our Moon is the biggest and brightest thing in the night sky.

BALL OF ROCK

The Moon is a huge ball of rock in space. It is so close to Earth that we can easily see light and dark marks on its surface.

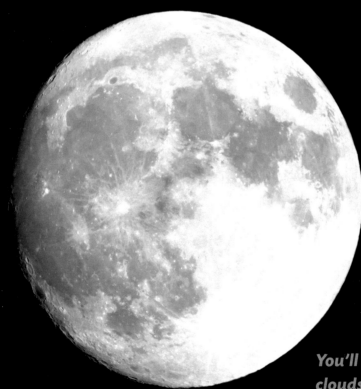

You'll never see clouds on the Moon, because the Moon has no atmosphere.

MOONLIGHT

The Moon shines brightly in the sky, but it doesn't give out any light of its own. It looks so bright because it reflects sunlight like a mirror.

Sunlight bouncing off the Moon takes just one second to reach Earth.

THE MOON'S FACE

From Earth, we always see the same side of the Moon. As it travels round the Earth it spins at exactly the right speed to keep the same side turned towards us.

SPOTLIGHT ON SPACE

THE MOON'S SEAS

Long ago, people thought the big dark parts of the Moon might be seas. Now we know they are places where rock melted and flowed across the Moon's surface.

BIG AND FAST

Our Moon is the fifth biggest of all the moons in the solar system. It travels through space around Earth about four times faster than a plane.

The Moon takes about a month to go round the Earth.

LOSING WEIGHT

The Moon is smaller than the Earth, so its pull of gravity is weaker than Earth's. Because of this, you would weigh less on the Moon than you do on Earth.

TURNING THE TIDE

The sea level on Earth rises and falls twice a day. These daily high and low tides are caused by the Moon pulling the sea towards it.

The tides on Earth are caused by the Moon's gravity.

7

HOW THE MOON BEGAN

Where did the Moon come from? Did it form separately from the Earth, or could it be part of the Earth that was flung out into space?

CRASH IN SPACE

About four and a half billion years ago, a world the size of Mars crashed into Earth. The rock thrown out into space gathered together and formed the Moon.

INSIDE THE MOON

The Moon has a small core made of iron. The core is surrounded by a thick layer of rock called the mantle. And the mantle is surrounded by a thin crust.

Crust · · · ·

Mantle · · · ·

Partly-melted core · · ·

Liquid outer core · · · ·

Solid inner core · · · ·

The centre of the Moon is hot enough to melt iron!

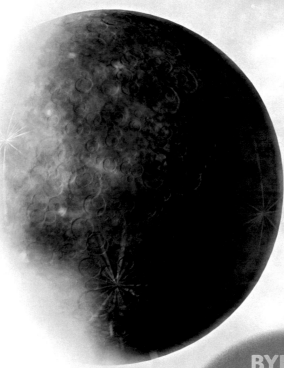

*The world that crashed into Earth
and created the Moon was called Theia.*

BYE BYE, MOON!

*When the Moon formed,
it was much closer to Earth.
Since then, it has been
drifting away from us.
Every year it moves
3.8 centimetres
further away.*

SPOTLIGHT ON SPACE

CHANGING SHAPE

Sometimes the Moon looks like a round disc. At other times, it seems to be a different shape. These shapes are called the phases of the Moon.

CHANGING SHAPE

Half of the Moon is lit by the Sun. The rest is invisible, in shadow. As the Moon orbits Earth, we see a different amount of its sunlit half each night.

The changing shape of the Moon is a trick of the light.

Shadows near the Moon's dark side show craters and mountains in great detail.

THE SHADOW LINE

The line between the light and dark sides of the Moon is called the terminator. Sunlight casts long shadows near the terminator, making bumps on the Moon's surface easier to see.

WAXING AND WANING

SPOTLIGHT ON SPACE

As the Moon grows bigger from night to night, we say it is waxing. Then, when it becomes smaller again, we say it is waning.

STUDYING THE MOON

People have gazed at the night sky for thousands of years. About 400 years ago, a new invention let them study it in more detail. This was the telescope.

A telescope makes the Moon look bigger as if it was closer.

MIRRORS AND LENSES

There are two types of telescopes, called refractors and reflectors. Refractors use lenses to make things look bigger. Reflectors use curved mirrors instead of lenses.

SPOTLIGHT ON SPACE

HARRIOT'S STUDY

The first person to study the Moon through a telescope was an English astronomer called Thomas Harriot. He pointed his telescope at the Moon on 26 July 1609.

Moon maps

People have made all sorts of different maps of the Moon. Some show where the mountains and craters are. Others show the different types of rocks on the Moon's surface.

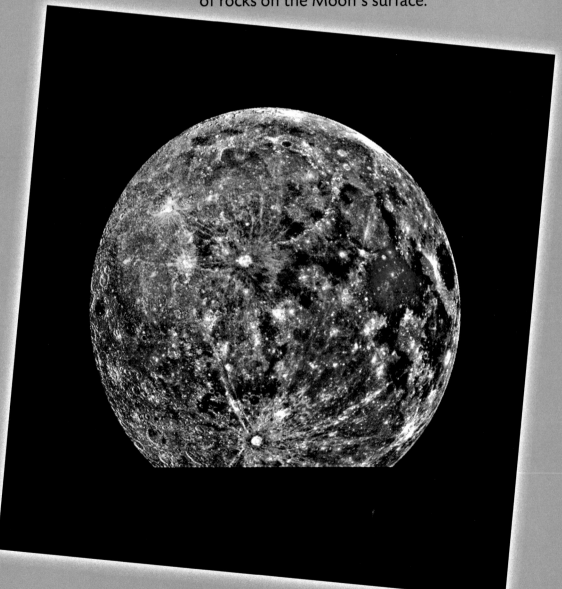

The colours in this map of the Moon show different types of rocks.

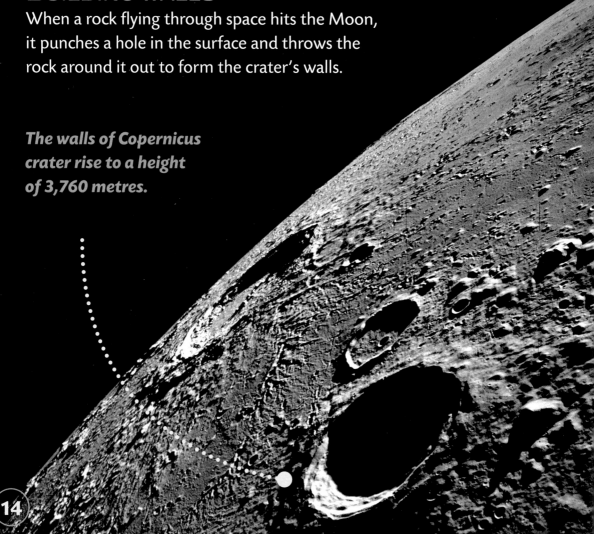

The Moon's Surface

The Moon's surface is covered with shallow holes called craters. They were made by rocks crashing into the Moon from space.

Building walls

When a rock flying through space hits the Moon, it punches a hole in the surface and throws the rock around it out to form the crater's walls.

The walls of Copernicus crater rise to a height of 3,760 metres.

MOUNTAIN PEAKS

SPOTLIGHT ON SPACE

*Big craters on the Moon
often have a mountain in
the middle. When the crater
was made, the middle was
pushed down so hard that
it bounced up and formed
the mountain.*

RAY CRATERS

Some of the Moon's
craters have bright
streaks called rays leading
away from them. The
rays are light-coloured
rock and dust thrown out
on to the dark surface
when the crater formed.

Exploring the Moon

Dozens of unmanned spacecraft and astronauts have explored the Moon. Twelve astronauts landed on the Moon and brought Moon rocks back to Earth.

Moonwalk

The first person ever to walk on the Moon was US astronaut Neil Armstrong (1930-2012). He landed on the Moon's Sea of Tranquillity with Buzz Aldrin on 20 July 1969.

Apollo 11 astronaut Buzz Aldrin stands on the dusty surface of the Moon.

UNLUCKY 13

*The Apollo 13 spacecraft
exploded on its way to the
Moon in 1970. Amazingly,
the three astronauts were
able to fly the damaged
spacecraft round the
Moon and back
to Earth.*

MOON BUGGY

The last three manned
spaceflights to the Moon took
an electric car called a lunar rover
with them. Nicknamed the Moon
buggy, it let the astronauts travel
further from their spacecraft.

*Each lunar rover had seats
for two astronauts wearing
bulky spacesuits.*

THE MOON'S FAR SIDE

From Earth, we always see the same side of the Moon. The other side was a mystery until a spacecraft took the first photograph of it in 1959.

LOOKS DIFFERENT

The far side of the Moon looks very different from the side we see from Earth. It has a lot more craters and just a few tiny seas.

Many spacecraft have photographed and mapped the Moon's far side.

NAMING CRATERS

The many craters on the near side of the Moon are named after famous astronomers and scientists from long ago. Craters on the far side are named after people from more recent times.

Plaskett is a crater on the far side of the Moon.

The *Lunar Reconnaissance* **Orbiter** *was sent to map the Moon in 2009.*

BUILDING ON THE MOON

SPOTLIGHT

Astronomers think the far side of the Moon would be a great place to build telescopes, but it would cost a lot of money and be difficult to do.

Eclipses

The Sun, Moon and Earth sometimes line up in a row. The result is an eclipse. There are solar eclipses and lunar eclipses. Every year, there are about three eclipses.

Casting shadows

A lunar eclipse happens when the Earth moves between the Sun and Moon. The Earth casts a shadow on part of the Moon or all of it.

FLAT EARTH?

If you didn't know what shape the Earth is, you could find out by looking at the Moon during a lunar eclipse. You can see the shadow of Earth's round shape on the Moon.

Earth casts its round shadow on the Moon during a partial lunar eclipse.

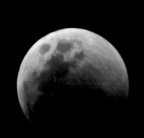

The Moon turns red during a total lunar eclipse.

SOLAR ECLIPSES

A solar eclipse happens when the Moon moves between the Earth and Sun. The Moon covers part of the Sun or all of it, turning day into night.

SPOTLIGHT ON SPACE

GLOSSARY

astronaut A space traveller.

astronomer A scientist who studies the Universe beyond Earth.

atmosphere The gases that surround a star, planet or moon.

billion A thousand million.

core The centre of a star, planet or moon.

craters Shallow holes in the surface of a planet or moon, caused by pieces of rock hitting the surface or by a volcano erupting.

crust The surface of a planet like Earth, made of rock.

Earth The planet we live on, the third planet from the Sun.

eclipse The hiding from view, or dimming, of an object in the sky when something else passes in front of it.

gravity A force that pulls things towards a star, planet, moon or other large object.

mantle The part of a planet or moon between the core and the crust.

Mars The fourth planet from the Sun, also called the red planet because of its colour.

orbit The path of a planet, spacecraft or moon around a larger body.

phases of the Moon The shape of the sunlit part of the Moon that changes from night to night.

planet A large world in orbit around the Sun or another star.

reflector A type of telescope that uses curved mirrors to make a magnified image.

refractor A type of telescope that uses lenses to make a magnified image.

solar system The Sun and all the planets, moons and other bodies that travel through space with it.

telescope An instrument used by astronomers to make faraway objects in the sky look closer and bigger.

terminator The line between the sunlit half and dark half of a planet or moon.

tides The twice-daily rise and fall of the sea caused by the Moon's pull of gravity.

WEBSITES

http://science.howstuffworks.com/lunar-landing.htm
Find out how the Apollo Moon landings worked.

http://school.familyeducation.com/astronautics/moon/38470.html
Lots to read about Moon rocks brought back to Earth by the Apollo astronauts.

http://www.sciencekids.co.nz/sciencefacts/space/moon.html
Have a look at these fun facts about the Moon.

http://www.spacekids.co.uk/moon/
Find out about the Apollo Moon landings from the US space agency NASA.

http://www.bbc.co.uk/science/space/solarsystem/space_missions/luna_9
Read about the Soviet space probe, *Luna 9*, which made the first controlled landing on the Moon in 1966.

http://www.bbc.co.uk/science/space/solarsystem/space_missions/ranger_program
A series of spacecraft called *Ranger* were sent to the Moon to prepare the way for the first astronauts.

http://www.planetsforkids.org/moon-moon.html
Lots more facts about the Moon.

INDEX